PRAYERS

God Always Answers

For Forgiveness

Publications International, Ltd.

Cover art: Shutterstock.com

Interior art: Art Explosion, Clipart.com, Dover, Shutterstock.com

Scripture quotations from *The Holy Bible, King James Version*. Copyright © 1977, 1984, Thomas Nelson, Inc., Publishers.

Louis Weber, CEO
Publications International, Ltd.
8140 Lehigh Avenue
Morton Grove, IL 60053

Permission is never granted for commercial purposes.

ISBN: 978-1-68022-706-2

Manufactured in China.

8 7 6 5 4 3 2 1

INTRODUCTION

Forgiveness is one of the toughest acts we humans are asked to perform, which is perhaps why we can be so skeptical of God's infinite capacity of forgiveness. How can that be true, when we have trouble moving on from a neighbor's irritating behavior or a snide remark from a relative? Prayer lets each of us speak candidly with God about our struggles to forgive others and ourselves. We ask for God's help to boost our own capacity to forgive while asking for his forgiveness in turn.

For if ye forgive men their trespasses, your heavenly Father will also forgive you: But if ye forgive not men their trespasses, neither will your Father forgive your trespasses.

— Matthew 6:15–16

Here in Matthew we find the absolute key to success in our prayers for forgiveness: we must forgive in order to ask God to forgive. Christian thinkers have written about this very issue for nearly two thousand years because of the sheer challenge of it. We can find strength in Scripture and in the words of those who came before us, and we can find the best way to ask for God's help as we seek to "forgive those who trespass against us.

Although the fig tree shall not blossom, neither shall fruit be in the vines; the labour of the olive shall fail, and the fields shall yield no meat; the flock shall be cut off from the fold, and there shall be no herd in the stalls: Yet I will rejoice in the Lord, I will joy in the God of my salvation.

— *Habakkuk 3:17-18*

✠ ✠ ✠

Life is not easy; in fact, some days, even arising to face the day is a truly daunting task. Because sin entered the world and corrupted God's perfect design, we may find ourselves bruised like fragile reeds by the painful effects of a broken world. If we allow ourselves to stay in our broken state without relying on the powerful source of God's comfort, peace, and love, we might even find ourselves as hopeless as a smoldering wick about to lose its flame.

O Lord my God, I cried unto thee, and thou hast healed me.

✠ ✠ ✠

The state of hopelessness is dangerous; it is one of the worst places to allow ourselves to dwell. However, God knows our heartache, and he understands our suffering. When we have been bruised in this world, he offers us healing. We may never understand why we have to encounter heartbreaking experiences, but we can hold securely to the truth that God's justice is certain. He will heat our hearts with the flame of his joy again.

*F*or this shall every one that is godly
pray unto thee in a time when thou
mayest be found: surely in the floods of
great waters they shall not come nigh
unto him.

— *Psalm 32:5*

✝ ✝ ✝

An honest man is not a man who never lies.
There is no such man. When an honest man
is caught in a lie or discovers he has lied, he
is quick to admit it. He then speaks the truth.
He's not afraid to say, "Please forgive me for
not being honest." He does not defend a lie.
Unlike a dishonest man, he does not make
plans to lie or use lies to cover other false-
hoods. He regularly scrutinizes his life to see
if he has lied or is living a lie in any area. He
approaches God with an open heart and asks

to be forgiven. Even in trials and tribulations, God listens and forgives.

*A*nd he believed in the Lord; and he counted it to him for righteousness.

— Genesis 15:6

✠ ✠ ✠

We need to pass on to our children and remind ourselves that if we have deep convictions — convictions that have not just been handed to us, but that have been seared into our souls through difficult battles won — those convictions will be tested. They will be tried in the fires of outside pressures. I am not certain that a conviction is a worthwhile one if it is not tested and tried in the refining fires of life experiences and human opposition.

Wherefore, my beloved brethren,
let every man be swift to hear,
slow to speak, slow to wrath:
For the wrath of man worketh not the
righteousness of God.

— James 1:19–20

✠ ✠ ✠

God, as much as I don't want to, I can't help
but listen to your love, which calls me to
always seek to make my enemies my friends.
How I have grown to truly dislike the call of
this love! I would rather love a stranger than
an enemy. This is not easy to even want to do!
Still, I know that this is what you want me to
do in order to make your love real in my life.
And so, Lord, flood me with your love because
this call is a hard one for me. Amen.

B ut do thou for me, O God the Lord, for thy name's sake: because thy mercy is good, deliver thou me.

— *Psalms 109:21*

✠ ✠ ✠

Psalm 109 is a scorcher, famous for its salt-the-earth language about one's enemies. Its author reaches for God to confirm his faith and prove those enemies wrong. God sets an example of mercy and charity that we can easily spend our lives trying to emulate. To always be kind and generous is an intimidating idea, but to make one kind or generous choice at a time is so doable.

They bowed themselves with their faces to the ground upon the pavement, and worshipped, and praised the Lord, saying, For he is good; for his mercy endureth for ever.

— 2 Chronicles 7:3

Solomon appears in so much of the Old Testament, casting a long shadow as a wise, powerful, wealthy leader favored by God. Even so, he and his people have sins and flaws to atone for. The most powerful people still have to answer to God, but they can also ask for God's help. Solomon acts as a role model for his people.

For we know him that hath said, Vengeance belongeth unto me, I will recompense, saith the Lord. And again, The Lord shall judge his people. It is a fearful thing to fall into the hands of the living God.

— *Hebrews* 10:30–31

✠ ✠ ✠

Only God can judge — we all know this cornerstone of scripture and do our flawed best to honor it. But how interesting to think of "the living God." When Jesus Christ was on Earth, his disciples not only learned from his example; they made choices and lived their lives in his presence. Imagine if God were standing, bodily, next to every person you met. How might you act differently?

*Sing, O heavens; and be joyful,
O earth; and break forth into
singing, O mountains: for the Lord hath
comforted his people, and will have
mercy upon his afflicted.*

— *Isaiah 49:13*

✠ ✠ ✠

Isaiah wants his prophecy of mercy and joy to
be contagious for all of creation: the people as
well as the heavens and the mountains. It's a
touching counterpoint to the times when God
shakes the earth to show his people the error
of their ways. Isaiah's prophecy, echoing
Psalm 100, reminds us to express our gratitude
and love to God.

I have blotted out, as a thick cloud, thy transgressions, and, as a cloud, thy sins: return unto me; for I have redeemed thee.

— *Isaiah 44:22*

✠ ✠ ✠

Is there a burden or grudge you carry with you? Imagine the same thick cloud engulfing it and sweeping it out of your mind. Ask God to help you forgive and move on.

I f our failure teaches us to turn afresh to Him, and find in Him the grace He gives to pray as we ought, this humiliation may become our greatest blessing.

— Rev. Andrew Murray

A nd I say unto you, Ask, and it shall be given you; seek, and ye shall find; knock, and it shall be opened unto you.

— Luke 11:9

✠ ✠ ✠

You may be afraid to ask for what you want. Think of it this way: Someone who knows you and loves you will probably choose gifts that you like, but you might need to tell them about the gift you'd really love to get.

*L*et your conversation be without covetousness; and be content with such things as ye have: for he hath said, I will never leave thee, nor forsake thee.

— *Hebrews 13:5*

✠ ✠ ✠

Like an ersatz wedding invitation, God's presence is present enough. Think about an item you wish you had — a newer car, a bigger house — and imagine all the better "things unseen" that you have instead.

A Christian may often have very earnest desires for spiritual blessings. But alongside of these there are other desires in his daily life occupying a large place in his interests and affections. The spiritual desires are not all-absorbing. He wonders that his prayer is not heard. It is simply that God wants the whole heart.

— Rev. Andrew Murray

F or we are his workmanship, created in Christ Jesus unto good works, which God hath before ordained that we should walk in them.

— *Ephesians 2:10*

✠ ✠ ✠

Think about a person who helped to guide you to follow in God's footsteps, or perhaps guided you back to them after you'd wandered off the path. Who helped that person find their way to God? Even now, thousands of years later, to follow Christ involves the same word of mouth as the epistle to the Ephesians.

Therefore I say unto you, What things soever ye desire, when ye pray, believe that ye receive them, and ye shall have them.

— Mark 11:24

✠ ✠ ✠

Children have an advantage in their relationship with God, because their thoughts are more clear and their conviction more pure.

As an adult, with so many obligations and complications, how do you quiet your other worries and doubts in order to talk to God with a clear mind?

L ooking back on the way by which we have come, it seems to me now that faith and work necessarily go together. Earnest believing prayer is not less earnest and believing because you use the means God has put within your reach. Your dependence upon God is just the same.

— Leonard K. Shaw

S earch me, O God, and know
my heart: try me, and know my
thoughts: And see if there be any wicked
way in me, and lead me in the way
everlasting.

— *Psalms 139:23–24*

✛ ✛ ✛

The psalmist sets a particularly good example
here: see me, God, and help me to improve.
What does God find when he searches you?

G race be to you, and peace, from God our Father, and from the Lord Jesus Christ.

— Ephesians 1:2

✠ ✠ ✠

All the epistles have beautiful greetings, specific to each audience. The Ephesians lived in a blended society, and Paul urges them to treat one another with deference and respect — perhaps hinted at here by his mention of peace. His message to coexist in the Lord is timeless.

B ut we are all as an unclean thing, and all our righteousnesses are as filthy rags; and we all do fade as a leaf; and our iniquities, like the wind, have taken us away.

— Isaiah 64:6

✠ ✠ ✠

To acknowledge humankind's nature as sinful beings, we must look frankly at ourselves; but we also have so much room to improve and strive and grow. A filthy rag is rinsed clean. A fallen leaf is replaced by a bright new bud. We walk against the wind until we reach home.

*A*nd when we cried unto the Lord, he heard our voice, and sent an angel, and hath brought us forth out of Egypt.

— Numbers 20:16

✠ ✠ ✠

My friend and I have had a falling out, Lord. The atmosphere is strained between us; the air is chilly. I don't know what I've said or done to cause this breach in our relationship. I only know we're at odds and my heart hurts. Relieve the anguish that I feel, Lord. Show me how to break the silence. Help me take the first step then you can do the rest. Heal us with your love.

A great many prayers are born of selfishness and are too much like dictation or command. None of God's promises are unconditional; and we have no such assets to our credit that we have a right to draw our cheques and demand that God shall pay them. The indispens- able quality of all right asking is a right spirit toward our heavenly Father. When a soul feels such an entire submissive- ness towards God that it delights in see- ing Him reign, and His glory advanced, it may fearlessly pour out its desires; for then the desires of God and the desires of that sincere submissive soul will agree. God loves to give to them who love to let

Him have His way; they find their happiness in the chime of their own desires with the will of God.

— Theodore L. Cuyler, D.D.

I n all things shewing thyself a pattern of good works: in doctrine shewing uncorruptness, gravity, sincerity, sound speech, that cannot be condemned.

— Titus 2:7-8

Blessed be the Lord, who daily loadeth us with benefits, even the God of our salvation.

— Psalm 68:19

✠ ✠ ✠

The house is a mess, Lord, and because of it, my attitude is a matching mood. Like handwriting on the wall of my grumpy heart, I got your message: 'Tis far wiser to hunt first crocuses on spring days than lost socks in the laundry; to sweep leaves into piles for jumping than grunge in a corner; to chase giggles rising from a child's soul like dandelion fluff than dust balls beneath beds. Bless, O Lord, this wonderful mess, and send me out to play.

L et us beware of the prayer for forgiveness becoming a formality: only what is really confessed is really forgiven. Such forgiveness, as a living experience, is impossible without a forgiving spirit to others: as forgiven expresses the heavenward, so forgiving the earthward, relation of God's child. In each prayer to the Father I must be able to say that I know of no one whom I do not heartily love.

— Henry Altemus

There is a place for tenderness; but when men are ground to powder by the judgment of God, tenderness is not manifest then. When the heart whispers "Spare" and justice says "Smite," men must obey the voice of justice, stifling the voice of the heart.

— Norman Maclean

I n returning and rest shall ye be saved; in quietness and in confidence shall be your strength.

— Isaiah 30:15

✠ ✠ ✠

Most of us realize that we are naturally self-centered, and we often respond to those around us in ways that make us appear proud, haughty, or arrogant. But if we look at Jesus's life, we see an excellent example of humility — an example that we should strive to follow. He taught that pride was destructive, but humility was powerful. Rather than touting His own greatness, Jesus was willing to kneel down and wash the feet of others, to show that we should all be servants to each other — and to God.

*A*nd *above all things have fervent charity among yourselves: for charity shall cover the multitude of sins.*

— 1 Peter 4:8

✠ ✠ ✠

Tonight there was a shooting star but I could not find it. There was no trail against the deep dusk. And as I mused at what I had seen, the "fixed fires" — the other stars — burned on. Some people, like shooting stars through our lives, are a wonderful presence that awakens our sleeping sense of adventure. Others are the stars that appear each night: always with us, faithful to the end.

Yes, my friends, there is but one way to obtain that armor of God, which will bring us safe through the battle of life; and that is, pray for it. Ask, and it shall be given to you; seek, and ye shall find; knock, and it shall be opened unto you. You who wish for true success in life, pray. Pray, if you never prayed before, morning and evening, with your whole hearts, for that Spirit of God which is truth, justice, peace, faith, and hope—and you shall not pray in vain.

— Charles Kingsley

*T*herefore we are buried with him by baptism into death: that like as Christ was raised up from the dead by the glory of the Father, even so we also should walk in newness of life.

— Romans 6:4

✠ ✠ ✠

Drawn like moths to flame, kids lead us new places. Guide me, pathfinding God, for I'm an aerialist leaping from bar to bar. For seconds, I'm holding neither old nor new: It's impossible to grasp a second bar while holding the first. Help me teach my children to swing on their own bars; to have standards, goals, a living faith. And help me to see, absorb, and forgive their growing pains and stumbles.

B ear ye one another's burdens, and so fulfil the law of Christ.

— *Galatians 6:2*

✠ ✠ ✠

Marriage does not ask that you completely lose yourself in the other person. Happy individuals make happy couples. Marriage does not demand that you think and act just like one another. Remember, it was your unique qualities that attracted you to each other in the first place. Marriage only requires that each of you becomes not someone else, but more of who you are already, only now you will become who you are together.

I will pray with the spirit, and I will pray with the understanding also: I will sing with the spirit, and I will sing with the understanding also.

— *1 Corinthians 14:15*

✠ ✠ ✠

The adage "Be careful what you wish for" is taken as a caution, but it's also good advice. The same prayer can come from a place of selflessness or of pride, and the difference is not only clear to God, it affects how we approach God in the first place. Pray with care and with a clear conscience. Be frank with God and be ready to receive a frank response.

How *precious also are thy thoughts unto me, O God! how great is the sum of them!*

— *Psalm 139:17*

✠ ✠ ✠

Sometimes I don't understand, God, although I know you always do what's best for me. My loved one has made a choice that hurts me. It's a riddle, O God, why you give us freedom to choose. It can break our hearts. Comfort me as I cope and guide me toward forgiveness. Help me separate doer from deed and be the bigger person. Help me remember that I sometimes make poor choices too.

Hereby perceive we the love of God, because he laid down his life for us: and we ought to lay down our lives for the brethren.

— 1 John 3:16

✠ ✠ ✠

We come today, O God, as near strangers gathered from scattered lives, for families no longer live close by. Be the common thread running through our reunion as we recall and rededicate our ancestors' memory. Bless us, Lord of history, the next generation. Bless and guide the young ones, our descendants. As we catch up with each other, embrace us and send us back to our distant homes renewed, refreshed, and revitalized until we once again join hands with you around the family table.

B e not rash with thy mouth, and let not thine heart be hasty to utter any thing before God: for God is in heaven, and thou upon earth: therefore let thy words be few.

— *Ecclesiastes 5:2*

✠ ✠ ✠

Remember that God is everything in the past, present, and future. We should choose to show reverence for his attentive ear and be mindful of how we express ourselves. God could never misapprehend us, but we can honor him with our words.

It is on prayer that the promises wait for their fulfilment, the kingdom for its coming, the glory of God for its full revelation. And for this blessed work, how slothful and unfit we are. It is only the Spirit of God can enable us to do it aright.

— Henry Altemus

He staggered not at the promise of God through unbelief; but was strong in faith, giving glory to God; And being fully persuaded that, what he had promised, he was able also to perform.

— Romans 4:20–21

✠ ✠ ✠

We are far too easily pleased, Lord. We run after our toys with such vigor. We work and work, earning more and more money, thinking that somehow happiness can be bought, or that the joy of the future can be mortgaged today. But your promise is not found on the "fast track." We must open our hearts and give ourselves over to your word. Give us that vision, God, and the determination to reach for your promises every day.

And even when we know what to ask, how much there is still needed to make prayer acceptable. It must be to the glory of God, in full surrender to His will, in full assurance of faith, in the name of Jesus, and with a perseverance that, if need be, refuses to be denied. All this must be learned.

— Henry Altemus

In our intercourse with God the difficulty is not on His side, but on ours.

— Rev. Andrew Murray

F or whom the Lord loveth he chasteneth, and scourgeth every son whom he receiveth. If ye endure chastening, God dealeth with you as with sons; for what son is he whom the father chasteneth not?

— *Hebrews 12:6–7*

✠ ✠ ✠

God sets an example of all-encompassing love that includes discipline. We struggle when our children or other family members misbehave or when coworkers treat us badly. Is there someone in your life you should treat more strictly? Is there someone to whom you should express your needs more clearly?

Yes, the deeper the need, and the more bitter the extremity, the greater the opportunity for God to show forth his mighty power in our lives, if we but give him a chance by unswerving obedience at any cost.

— Rosalind Goforth

He that covereth a transgression seeketh love; but he that repeateth a matter separateth very friends.

— *Proverbs 17:9*

✠ ✠ ✠

No matter how hard I try, God of patience and support, someone finds fault with me. I am mortified about the latest criticism. Give me the courage to confront this, Lord, for it is not acceptable to be treated this way even when in error. Keep me calm, factual, and open; perhaps the tone was unintentional, the critic unaware of the power of shaming. Help me remember how I feel now the next time I find fault with someone. Truth be known, Lord, such abrasive manners say more about the criticizer than the criticized. Keep me from passing them on.

S ome have asked, "But have you never sinned?" Yes, I grieve to say I have. Sin is the one thing I abhor—for it is the one thing that can, if unrepented of, separate us, not from Christ, but from the consciousness of his presence. But I have learned that there is instantaneous forgiveness and restoration to be had always. That there need be no times of despair.

— Rosalind Goforth

A nd wherever faith has accepted the Father's love, obedience accepts the Father's will.

— Henry Altemus

*G*ive unto the Lord, ye kindreds of the people, give unto the Lord glory and strength. Give unto the Lord the glory due unto his name: bring an offering, and come before him: worship the Lord in the beauty of holiness.

— 1 Chronicles 16:28-29, 34

✠ ✠ ✠

Carpe diem—how's that for a motto, Lord? It invites me to forgive past errors, prioritize my to-do lists, and take steps today toward the rest of my life. What will endure? Time I gave the committees instead of family and self? Chores I did instead of picnicking, listening to a child's story, resting by a winding stream? Lord, your word inspires me not only to seize the day but to cherish it.

I exhort therefore, that, first of all, supplications, prayers, intercessions, and giving of thanks, be made for all men.

— *1 Timothy 2:1*

✠ ✠ ✠

Each kind of prayer is important, and all of humankind deserves those prayers. We pray for those in need, whether we know them personally or not; but we must also pray for those who have great power and privilege. How should our prayers for these groups differ in tone and spirit?

O r let him take hold of my strength,
that he may make peace with me.
— *Isaiah 27:5*

✠ ✠ ✠

God speaks of Israel as a vine to be nurtured,
and a vine must have support in order to climb
and thrive. We're surrounded by these outposts
of God, these potential sources of strength,
toward which we can reach and grow.

G od forbid that I should sin against the Lord in ceasing to pray for you.

— 1 Samuel 12:23

✠ ✠ ✠

Samuel's comment can seem like a nicety as he says goodbye to the Israelites, but his fear of God is very real. The Israelites demanded a king; God agreed but made sure they knew, in words and with thunder, that they'd been sinful to question God. Samuel must pray for them as both a believer and a prophet.

*G*od is faithful, who will not suffer you to be tempted above that ye are able; but will with the temptation also make a way to escape, that ye may be able to bear it.

— *1 Corinthians 10:13*

✠ ✠ ✠

I never meant to be a failure, Lord, never meant to break commitments, but I am and I did. Please comfort me, for I mourn this failure and its repercussions to my loved ones. I mourn for the person I pledged to be. Forgive my failures and help me to forgive myself and move on with courage. Help me grieve and move on from these toxic feelings.

For God sent not his Son into the world to condemn the world; but that the world through him might be saved. He that believeth on him is not condemned: but he that believeth not is condemned already, because he hath not believed in the name of the only begotten Son of God.

— 1 John 3:16-17

✠ ✠ ✠

The love and devotion of family serves as the foundation upon which faith is built and cherished. The support of family acts both as wings to fly and a safety net to catch us. The honesty and trustworthiness of family creates both sanctuary and accountability for each of us in our journeys.

F or thine eyes are open upon all the ways of the sons of men: to give every one according to his ways, and according to the fruit of his doings.

— Jeremiah 32:19

✠ ✠ ✠

Think of someone you respect and admire, and imagine their "ways and doings" listed alongside your own. How do the lists compare and contrast? There is probably an opportunity to improve hiding in your daily routine.

*A*nd for those who know not Christ?
For them, too, we can pray. For,
for them too Christ died. They, too,
belong to Christ, for he has bought them
with his most precious blood.

— Charles Kingsley

*W*oe to the rebellious children,
saith the Lord, that take counsel,
but not of me.

— Isaiah 30:1

✠ ✠ ✠

When we need advice, it can be tempting to
comparison shop, like a child asking a fortune-
telling toy the same question over and over.
Often our gut instinct tells us the right
answer, informed by our relationship with
God, our morals, and our values.

Think of God in His infinite majesty, His altogether incomprehensible glory, His unapproachable holiness, sitting on a throne of grace, waiting to be gracious, inviting, encouraging you to pray with His promise: "Call upon Me, and I will answer thee."

— Rev. Andrew Murray

L et, I pray thee, thy merciful kindness be for my comfort, according to thy word unto thy servant.

— Psalms 119:76

✠ ✠ ✠

We live in God's world and were made in his image, which means we're surrounded by chances to use our own merciful kindness. Like a muscle, this quality thrives on heavy lifting.

A nd when they had prayed, the place was shaken where they were assembled together; and they were all filled with the Holy Ghost, and they spake the word of God with boldness.

— Acts 3:31

Now the Lord is that Spirit: and where the Spirit of the Lord is, there is liberty.

— 2 Corinthians 3:17

✠ ✠ ✠

We have been guilty, Lord, of looking for our leaders in places of wealth and influence. We want to glorify the outwardly successful, passing over those who have learned to live wisely and with integrity. Rather, we tend to follow after those who give blithe answers with the appearance of absolute confidence. But you have offered us better, we know. Your spirit fills those who walk in humility, patience, and self-sacrifice. Please open our eyes that we may see those gentle faces beckoning us upward and onward in a spirit of love.

G od has so created us that the exercise of every healthy function causes joy. Prayer is meant to be as simple and natural as breathing or working to a healthy man. The reluctance we feel, and the failure we confess, are God's own voice calling us to acknowledge our disease, and to come to Him for the healing He has promised.

— Rev. Andrew Murray

He hath shewed thee, O man, what is good; and what doth the Lord require of thee, but to do justly, and to love mercy, and to walk humbly with thy God?

— Micah 6:8

✛ ✛ ✛

We have seen that inconceivable acts can cause our world to crumble around us. Yet we need not fall apart inside. If we place our trust in God's goodness, he will come to our aid and bring us comfort to restore our hope in the future. His love and compassion will lift our spirits so we can rejoice no matter what disaster or tragedy may befall us. For as long as God is beside us, nothing can defeat us or take what is truly important from us.

God never speaks to His people of sin except with a view to saving them from it. The same light that shows the sin will show the way out of it. The same power that breaks down and condemns will, if humbly yielded to and waited on in confession and faith, give the power to rise up and conquer.

— Rev. Andrew Murray

ow we exhort you, brethren, warn them that are unruly, comfort the feebleminded, support the weak, be patient toward all men.

— *1 Thessalonians 5:14*

✠ ✠ ✠

Lord, we need your help to move beyond the times we hurt one another and the times we willingly misunderstand; the times we assume we know all there is to know and turn away. And then there are the times that we make private rules only to publicly condemn anyone who fails to abide by them, limiting one another by labeling, interpreting, conditioning, insisting, resisting, defining. From all this, Lord, we come, asking that you forgive us as we forgive those "others" we need new eyes to see and ears to hear. Be with us as we do so.

O my God, I cry in the day time, but thou hearest not; and in the night season, and am not silent.

— Psalms 22:2

✠ ✠ ✠

This lament is poignant, but its message is uplifting: the psalmist wonders if God is listening yet prays to God about it. We relate to the psalmist's feelings and are inspired by his optimism.

B rethren, my heart's desire and prayer to God for Israel is, that they might be saved.

— Romans 10:1

✠ ✠ ✠

Paul explains in careful detail how all people are still near to God and can easily take the final step toward Jesus Christ. He wades deep into theology but never loses sight of his personal relationship with God and his fellow man. He remembers his past as someone who persecuted Christians and has compassion.

Pray to him, that he may take possession of all your thoughts, feelings, and desires, and purge you from every taint of selfishness. Give up your hearts to him; and grieve not, by any selfishness, passion, or hardness of your own, his gracious instructions: but let him teach you, and guide you, and purge you, and sanctify you, till you come to the stature of a perfect man, to the fulness of the measure of Christ, who could perfectly hate the sin, and yet perfectly love the sinner; who could see in every man, even in his enemies and murderers, a friend and a brother.

— Charles Kingsley

Turn ye unto me, saith the Lord of hosts, and I will turn unto you.

— *Zechariah 1:3*

✠ ✠ ✠

Is an opportunity waiting for you to "put yourself out there"? A setback or bad decision can lead us to hesitate before God, as though he only loves us when our behavior is flawless.

J ust because your heart is cold and prayerless, get you into the presence of the loving Father. As a father pitieth his children, so the Lord pitieth you. Do not be thinking of how little you have to bring God, but of how much He wants to give you. Just place yourself before, and look up into, His face; think of His love, His wonderful, tender, pitying love. Just tell Him how sinful and cold and dark all is: it is the Father's loving heart will give light and warmth to yours.

— Henry Altemus

The people that walked in darkness have seen a great light: they that dwell in the land of the shadow of death, upon them hath the light shined.

— *Isaiah 9:2*

✠ ✠ ✠

Television isn't the place to look for sincerity, but I can feel tempted by the ministries of those who claim God smiles on us with earthly wealth. Every day we work hard for what seems like less and less, and I look to you, Lord, for answers why I'm not more successful, why my family struggles, why so many others have so much more. Please help me to remember that money may be here and now but your kingdom is forever and ever.

The more we pray, and the more conscious we become of our unfitness to pray in power, the more we shall be urged and helped to press on towards the secret of power in prayer — a life abiding in Christ entirely at His disposal.

— Rev. Andrew Murray

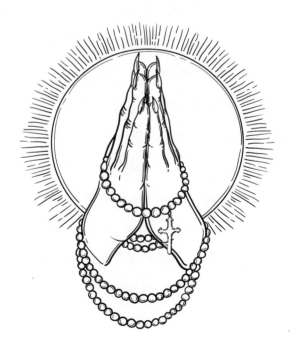

I t is good for me that I have been afflicted; that I might learn thy statutes.

— *Psalms 119:71*

There's a paradox in learning from our mistakes, because we have to be able to see and understand them as mistakes in order to glean the lesson. And it's always as humbling as it was the first time.

W hen we enter a store or shop
we ask the salesman to hand
us the particular article we want. The
model prayers mentioned in the Bible
were short and right to the mark. "God
be merciful to me a sinner!" "Lord, save
me!" cries sinking Peter. "Come down,
ere my child die!" exclaims the heart-
stricken nobleman.

— Theodore L. Cuyler, D.D.

For the promise is unto you, and to your children, and to all that are afar off, even as many as the Lord our God shall call.

— Acts 2:39

✠ ✠ ✠

Christians cover the world, as "afar off" as anyone could get. But think about the spiritual distance that grows between us and God when we're stretched too thin or simply don't want to reach for him. How can we narrow that gap?

P ray to him, that he may take possession of all your thoughts, feelings, and desires, and purge you from every taint of selfishness. Give up your hearts to him; and grieve not, by any selfishness, passion, or hardness of your own, his gracious instructions: but let him teach you, and guide you, and purge you, and sanctify you, till you come to the stature of a perfect man, to the fulness of the measure of Christ, who could perfectly hate the sin, and yet perfectly love the sinner; who could see in every man, even in his enemies and murderers, a friend and a brother.

— Charles Kingsley

Y et I will rejoice in the Lord, I will
joy in the God of my salvation.

— *Habakkuk 3:18*

✠ ✠ ✠

We're stained, like a paint rag, by troubles we
caused ourselves, Lord. Red, the color of lost
temper and rudeness. Green, envy of others
who have it easier and more of it. Blue, the
shade of despair over something we could
change. Yellow, of cowardly running.
Rearrange our unsightly smudges into glorious
rainbows through your gift of forgiveness.

When thou vowest a vow unto God, defer not to pay it; for he hath no pleasure in fools: pay that which thou hast vowed.

✠ ✠ ✠

We have all been hurt in life. We have all been at the receiving end of another's wrath or anger. Even if that person never apologizes, we must still forgive. Do we want to live our lives holding onto the actions of another? Do we want to feel the tension of another person's behaviors towards us? It is only when we forgive that we can once again feel light and loving and kind.

God offers Himself, gives Himself away, to the whole-hearted who give themselves wholly away to Him. He always gives us according to our heart's desire. But not as we think it, but as He sees it.

— Rev. Andrew Murray

We are carnal and cannot bring God the worship He seeks. But Jesus came to give the Spirit: He has given Him to us.

— Henry Altemus

For neither at any time used we flattering words, as ye know, nor a cloke of covetousness; God is witness: Nor of men sought we glory, neither of you, nor yet of others, when we might have been burdensome, as the apostles of Christ.

— 1 Thessalonians 2:5–6

✠ ✠ ✠

If I forgive someone, I am not doing it just for that person, but for myself. The weight of holding onto things that have been done to me dampens my spirit. When I forgive, that weight is lifted and I no longer feel connected to what was done to me. The person I forgive is free as well. It's all about letting go of the things that drag me down so I can live the life God intended.

A good and wise father must often deny his child the article for which he asks, but he will not dismiss the matter with a curt denial. He will try to find something else for his child.

— Russell H. Conwell

The pull of our prayer may not move the everlasting throne, but— like the pull on a line from the bow of a boat—it may draw us into closer fellowship with God.

— Theodore L. Cuyler, D.D.

Yea, the darkness hideth not from thee; but the night shineth as the day: the darkness and the light are both alike to thee. For thou hast possessed my reins: thou hast covered me in my mother's womb.

— *Psalms 139:12–13*

✠ ✠ ✠

Lord, only you can take all the heartaches and failures in our lives and turn them into compassionate messages of hope for others. We care for an aging parent who passes away, and so are able to relate to the needs of the elderly around us. We go through a divorce, and we can then give genuine advice during our interactions with single mothers. Our pain becomes others' gain, Lord. Sometimes looking back over our shoulders brings us hope for the opportunities that are surely ahead of us. Thank you for second chances.

G od loves to give to them who love to let Him have His way; they find their happiness in the chime of their own desires with the will of God.

— Theodore L. Cuyler, D.D.

Deal bountifully with thy servant,
that I may live, and keep thy word.

— Psalms 119:17

✠ ✠ ✠

We pray for the health of each family member.
You know our bodies better than we do. Every
ache and pain, every sickness, is a concern to
you. Therefore we ask that you keep watch
over our bones and muscles and every bodily
system, because you are the Great Healer. We
ask for guidance in all the decisions we must
make in the days ahead, the big decisions, and
even the little daily ones. We acknowledge
that without divine direction, our lives
become meaningless, wrapped up in our own
selfishness, heading nowhere. Lead us where
you want us to go!

So in all things, that which God has given me intelligence and power to do, in avoiding evil or securing good, I am under direct command from him to do, always depending upon His blessing to secure the needed result. A true faith in God will be made manifest by careful obedience to known commands. An intelligent faith can never allow dependence upon means used to take the place of dependence upon the living God.

— D.W. Whittle

Remember them that are in bonds, as bound with them; and them which suffer adversity, as being yourselves also in the body.

— Hebrews 13:3

✠ ✠ ✠

I am thankful to the Lord for His gift of forgiveness. I know I am not perfect and I know I make mistakes. Grant me the wisdom and grace to know when I am wrong and to ask for forgiveness. Give me a sense of gratitude toward those who forgive my errors, and help me forgive others who have offended me.

Thou knowest my downsitting and mine uprising, thou understandest my thought afar off.

— Psalms 139:2

✠ ✠ ✠

My closest friends, dear Lord, are a reprieve for my soul. Their acceptance sets me free to be myself. Their unconditional love forgives my failings. Thank you for these people who are a reflection of your love in my life. Help me be a friend who will lay down my life in such loving ways.

And though the Lord give you the bread of adversity, and the water of affliction, yet shall not thy teachers be removed into a corner any more, but thine eyes shall see thy teachers: And thine ears shall hear a word behind thee, saying, This is the way, walk ye in it, when ye turn to the right hand, and when ye turn to the left.

— Isaiah 30:20–21

✠ ✠ ✠

Lord, let me be strong today, drawing my courage from my hope in you. Help me lean not on my own strength but on your limitless power. I know there is work to be done— burdens to be lifted, temptations to be resisted, unkindness to be forgiven. Let my thoughts and actions be motivated by the hope generated by your promises.

T ake quiet time, and be still before
God, that He may take this matter
in hand. Leave yourself in God's hands.
— Rev. Andrew Murray

T he trusting believer in prayer rests
in God in a peaceful condition of soul.
— Russell H. Conwell

If ye abide in me, and my words abide in you, ye shall ask what ye will, and it shall be done unto you.

— John 15:7

✠ ✠ ✠

Dear God, why is it often the people closest to us that hurt us the most? Today I ask for the strength to deal with difficult people in the way you would want me to. Today I ask for the ability to find it in my heart to forgive them their trespasses, as I would hope they'd forgive mine. Today I ask for enough love to look beyond their problems and see them as you see them, as human beings deserving of love and care, even if I have to do it from a distance. Help me to forgive and move on, God. Amen.

And for those who know not Christ? What will happen to them we know not: but this we know, that they are his sheep, lost sheep though they may be; and that we are bound to pray, that he would bring them home to his flock.

— Charles Kingsley

That Christ may dwell in your hearts by faith; that ye, being rooted and grounded in love, May be able to comprehend with all saints what is the breadth, and length, and depth, and height; And to know the love of Christ, which passeth knowledge, that ye might be filled with all the fulness of God.

— *Ephesians 3:17–19*

✠ ✠ ✠

God, I ask in prayer for your forgiveness. I've not been the most loving and kind person lately, and I've treated people terribly as a result. I plan to reach out to each and every one of them and ask their forgiveness, but first I come to you in hopes that you will help me be a better person, a more loving and caring friend, and someone who treats others as I'd like to be treated. Please take away the defects in me that cause me to do harm to others, and strengthen the good qualities I have. I am a loving person, but when life backs me into a corner, I know I can be awful. Please forgive me and empower me to make better choices in the future and be the person you want me to be. Amen.

The direct answers to prayers of which I could tell you would fill a volume. I have always asked God for a definite gift for a definite purpose, and God has always given it to me.

— William Quarrier

B ut ye, beloved, building up yourselves on your most holy faith, praying in the Holy Ghost, Keep yourselves in the love of God, looking for the mercy of our Lord Jesus Christ unto eternal life.

— Jude 20–21

✠ ✠ ✠

Do not worry about the regrets of the past. God forgives you. Do not stress over a wrong word or a misguided action. God forgives you. Do not cry over a bad decision or a terrible mistake. God forgives you. Learn the lessons from your actions, then turn to God and know that he loves you and forgives you. Then strive to do better the next time.

The little child may ask of the father only what it needs for itself; and yet it soon learns to say, Give some for sister too. But the grown-up son, who only lives for the father's interest and takes charge of the father's business, asks more largely, and gets all that is asked.

— Henry Altemus

In the Lord's Prayer, in the parables on prayer, in the illustration of a child asking bread, of our seeking and knocking, in the central thought of the prayer of faith—everywhere our Lord urges and encourages us to offer definite petitions, and to expect definite answers.

— Rev. Andrew Murray

S *hall any teach God knowledge?*
— Job 21:22

✠ ✠ ✠

To forgive someone is the highest form of compassion. To try and understand that another's actions might have come from their own anger or struggles means we are empathic towards our fellow humans. God forgives us and offers his compassion. Why would we not do the same to our fellow humans?

And fill me, Lord, with the confidence that with such a teacher as Thou art I shall learn to pray. In the assurance that I have as my teacher, Jesus, who is ever praying to the Father, and by His prayer rules the destinies of His Church and the world, I will not be afraid. As much as I need to know of the mysteries of the prayer-world, Thou wilt unfold for me. And when I may not know, Thou wilt teach me to be strong in faith, giving glory to God.

— Henry Altemus

Trust in him at all times; ye people, pour out your heart before him: God is a refuge for us.

— Psalms 62:8

✠ ✠ ✠

How blessed we are to have the mercy and forgiveness of God! No matter what we do, God is ready to love and forgive us. This doesn't mean we go out and purposely do wrong, thinking we will get away with it, but we are human, and we do make mistakes now and then. Knowing that God won't abandon us when we do keeps us humble.

O give thanks unto the Lord, for he is good: for his mercy endureth for ever.

— *Psalms 107:1*

✠ ✠ ✠

Holding onto anger poisons the spirit. We must learn to let go and let God remove the anger so that we can feel free. Release the burden to God through forgiveness. Just because we forgive doesn't mean we condone the behavior, just that we no longer allow it to control us. Give it to God. Forgive.

As Mary faced the forest, now dark and mysterious, and filled with the noises of night, a feeling of helplessness and fear came over her. What unseen perils might she not meet? What would she find at the end? How would she be received on this occasion? Her heart played the coward; she felt a desire to turn and flee. But she remembered that never in her life had God failed her, not once had there been cause to doubt the reality of His guidance and care. Still the shrinking was there; she could not even move her lips in prayer; she could only look up and utter inwardly one appealing word, "Father!"

— William Pringle Livingstone

Thus saith the Lord of hosts;
Consider your ways.

— *Haggai 1:7*

✠ ✠ ✠

Lord, help me to let go of the chains that bind
me to the people I cannot seem to forgive. I
pray for strength and wisdom to understand
that their sins against me were because of
their own deep fears. I pray for the guidance
to cut the chord that attaches me to them in
anger and the desire for revenge. Teach me to
forgive others, Lord, as you forgive me, and
to release the poison of resentment that takes
away my peace and serenity. Teach me to be
a better person and to recognize my own
humanity in others, even as I remove their
presence from my life. Amen.

Prayer is the greatest power God has put into our hands for service— praying is harder work than doing, at least I find it so, but the dynamic lies that way to advance the Kingdom.

— Mary Slessor

Our prayers are now for justice. Better far a righteous war than an immoral peace. We have been compelled to unsheath the sword, and we pray that no heart may falter, and no cry arise for the sheathing of the sword, until justice be done. Thus our prayers have become a cry for victory.—Norman Maclean

*A*nd when thou prayest, thou shalt not be as the hypocrites are: for they love to pray standing in the synagogues and in the corners of the streets, that they may be seen of men.

— Matthew 6:5

✠ ✠ ✠

God forgives me all of my sins and transgressions. In return, I am to forgive those who sin against me. This is hard to do, because it's so much easier to hold onto grudges and resentments, even over trivial things. I feel that I was right and just, and that they hurt me. But until I can let go of that, I will never be free to be happy. God forgives me, and I must forgive others in return.

This, then, is our duty as to known dangers,—to guard ourselves against them by science, and the reason which God has given us; and as to unknown dangers, to pray to God to deliver us from them, if it seem good to him: but above all, to pray to him to deliver us from them in the best way, the surest way, the most lasting way, the way in which we may not only preserve ourselves, but our fellow-men and generations yet unborn; namely, by giving us wisdom and understanding to discover the dangers, to comprehend them, and to conquer them, by reason and by science.

— Charles Kingsley

*O*pen thou mine eyes, that I may behold wondrous things out of thy law.

— *Psalms 119:18*

✝ ✝ ✝

Have you ever felt the power of God's amazing grace? Have you ever tasted the sweetness of God's merciful forgiveness? Have you ever heard God's kind words of understanding and support? You will know it when you do, for all darkness will be made light, and all suffering will give way to a new joyfulness and inner peace. This is the power of God's amazing grace.

*B*ehold, the Lord's hand is not shortened, that it cannot save; neither his ear heavy, that it cannot hear: But your iniquities have separated between you and your God, and your sins have hid his face from you, that he will not hear.

— *Isaiah 59:1–2*

✠ ✠ ✠

Dear God, I don't come in prayer to you to ask for total forgiveness, even though I know you do forgive me my sins and mistakes. I ask that in addition to your merciful grace, you also help me to learn from my experience and glean wisdom from my interactions with the people I need to forgive, or need forgiveness from. Without this understanding, I fear I will repeat the same patterns in the future. Forgive me, God, then help me to forgive. But then, please, help me to increase my wisdom and come to a place in life where I don't keep repeating the same mistakes over and over again. Amen.

The human mind seems incapable of forming any other idea of God than can be obtained from a human model, greatly enlarged. Human kings, human fathers, human saints, human sinners are really pictured in the minds of all who strive to visualize the Almighty, or his Son, or the angels. No mind can meditate on nothing. Everything conceived in the mind must be like something else. So all those seemingly defeated ones had looked up to God as to a great man, and when he seemed to do nothing in answer to their requests they concluded that he either did not hear or that he would not even reply.

— *Russell H. Conwell*

L et us draw near with a true heart in full assurance of faith, having our hearts sprinkled from an evil conscience, and our bodies washed with pure water.

— *Hebrews 10:22*

✠ ✠ ✠

I know that when I am sad, lonely, and afraid, I can turn to God for his loving grace. With mercy and compassion, God hears my cries and comes to my aid, ready to take away my burdens and heal my wounded heart. He gives me wisdom and understanding, and helps me to forgive those who have hurt me. God's unceasing love for me is what grace is all about.

Hear, O heavens, and give ear, O earth: for the Lord hath spoken, I have nourished and brought up children, and they have rebelled against me.

— Isaiah 1:2

✠ ✠ ✠

Help me forgive my children for their mistakes, and understand that they are small and not yet mature in their behaviors. They don't misbehave because they are bad, but because they are children, and I ask that you always remind me that anything they break or mess up is not as important as making sure they know I love them. Please give me the patience to deal with them when they are bad, and the wisdom to let go of things that are truly not that important, even if I am angry or disappointed. Remind me, God, that I won't have my precious little ones forever, and to cherish and enjoy them while I can. Amen.

The more heartily we enter into the mind of our blessed Lord, and set ourselves simply just to think about prayer as He thought, the more surely will His words be as living seeds. They will grow and produce in us their fruit,—a life and practice exactly corresponding to the Divine truth they contain.

— Rev. Andrew Murray

Humble *yourselves in the sight of the Lord, and he shall lift you up.*

— James 4:10

✠ ✠ ✠

Someone may ask, "What's the difference between humility and humiliation?" A simple way to look at it is that humility is voluntary and peaceful, while humiliation is compulsory and painful. Practically speaking, it's better for me to think rightly about myself in relation to God and others (i.e., to walk in humility) than to think I'm "all that" and experience the humiliation of an extreme reality check. As I walk in true humility, there's the added bonus that God will send honor my way—and the honor he will set up for me will be sweeter than any I could try to grab for myself.

The friend who sincerely prays for you is a friend who would sacrifice most for you in case of need.

— Russell H. Conwell

Ye have wearied the Lord with your words. Yet ye say, Wherein have we wearied him?

— Malachi 2:17

✠ ✠ ✠

From scripture we learn to choose our words carefully when we talk to God, and to do this we have to be open to critique, even if it's only from ourselves.

If we expect a letter to reach its destination we put a stamp on it; otherwise it goes to the Dead-letter Office. There is what may be called a Dead-prayer Office, and thousands of well-worded petitions get buried up there. All of God's promises have their conditions; we must comply with those conditions, or we cannot expect the blessings coupled with the promises. In prayer, we must first be sure that we are doing our part if we expect God to do His part. There is a legitimate sense in which every Christian should do his utmost for the answering of his own prayers.

— Theodore L. Cuyler, D.D.

Continue in prayer, and watch in the same with thanksgiving; Withal praying also for us, that God would open unto us a door of utterance, to speak the mystery of Christ, for which I am also in bonds:

— Colossians 4:2–3

The brave and compassionate soul can forgive the most horrible of crimes. With God's love and guidance, we can forgive much less. People hurt people, and God asks that we look beyond the surface of things to the deeper truth. We are all God's children, even those that do terrible things, sometimes causing us tremendous pain and suffering. Forgive them anyway.

As we meditate on the words He spake on earth, let us yield ourselves to His teaching in the fullest confidence that, with such a teacher, we shall make progress.

— Henry Altemus

These all continued with one accord in prayer and supplication.

— Acts 1:14

✠ ✠ ✠

Lord, help us move beyond the times we hurt one another, the times we willingly misunderstand, the times we cherish our differences, and the times we assume we know all there is to know about each other and turn away. Amen.

Years ago there came to the Refuges the son of a man known to the Manchester police as "Mike the devil." Tom was as rough a customer as ever I saw, and for a time we had some trouble with him. But a great change came over him, and I have myself no doubt it was the result of personal pleading with God on his behalf. Tom is now an ordained minister of the Gospel in America. There is no end to the cases I could give of that kind. They all point to the same conclusion, that God does answer definite prayer. And today, after twenty-seven years of work, I praise Him for it.

— Leonard K. Shaw

Her priests have violated my law, and have profaned mine holy things: they have put no difference between the holy and profane, neither have they shewed difference between the unclean and the clean, and have hid their eyes from my sabbaths, and I am profaned among them.

— Ezekiel 22:26

Forgiveness is the first step to spiritual freedom. We cannot truly pray with an open heart if we are filled with malice toward ourselves or others.

Reveal therefore to me thy method, O Lord, and see whether I have followed it; that thou mayest have glory, if I have, and I pardon, if I have not, and help that I may.

— John Donne

With my whole heart have I sought thee: O let me not wander from thy commandments.

— *Psalms 119:10*

✠ ✠ ✠

Lord, we want to live life to its fullest. And although we know we shouldn't place our own wants before others' wants, it is so easy to think our dreams for the future matter most. Remind us to make compromises. Our love can get us further in this life than selfishness. Amen.

Servants of Christ! children of God! be of good courage. Let no fear of feebleness or poverty make you afraid— ask in the Name of Christ.

— Rev. Andrew Murray

But when ye pray, use not vain repetitions, as the heathen do: for they think that they shall be heard for their much speaking. Be not ye therefore like unto them: for your Father knoweth what things ye have need of, before ye ask him.

— Matthew 6:7–8

✠ ✠ ✠

Lord, bless us both in this time of separation. May we use the time wisely to consider our shortcomings, to seek ways to amend our faults, and to reconnect the relationship with a deeper love.

P rayer is to me the quick and instant recognition that all law is God's will, and all nature is in God's hand, and that all our welfare lies in linking ourselves with His will and placing ourselves in His hand through all the operations of the world and life and time.

— R.F. Horton, M.A., D.D.

I cried unto God with my voice, even unto God with my voice; and he gave ear unto me.

— Psalms 77:1

✠ ✠ ✠

Lord, I know that part of life is loss and that without loss we cannot treasure the new blessings that come our way. But I am still hurting, and the pain is deep. Help me see the beautiful silver lining that surrounds the dark clouds now hanging overhead. Amen.

God does not deal with all alike, either in His gifts of faith or in those of experience. We differ also in the use we make of His gifts.

— W. Boyd Carpenter, D.D.

When Jesus saw him lie, and knew that he had been now a long time in that case, he saith unto him, Wilt thou be made whole? The impotent man answered him, Sir, I have no man, when the water is troubled, to put me into the pool: but while I am coming, another steppeth down before me. Jesus saith unto him, Rise, take up thy bed, and walk. And immediately the man was made whole, and took up his bed, and walked.

— John 5:6–9

✠ ✠ ✠

After the storm, they cautiously push open their closet door and creep from their hiding place. How bad is it? They see destruction everywhere. Nothing left untouched, except for one safe spot—the closet in which the whole family crouched, pressed tight together, frightened, holding one another, praying. One thing remains, upright and safe—their hiding place in time of trouble, their sanctuary, the right place to be.

God is my Father, I am his child. As truly as I delight to be sought for by my child when he is cold or hungry, ill, or in need of protection, so is it with my Heavenly Father.

— Rosalind Goforth

And when ye stand praying, forgive, if ye have ought against any: that your Father also which is in heaven may forgive you your trespasses.

— Mark 11:25

Father, I know that I am not perfect, but please help me accept my shortcomings. Give me the wings of infinite spirit, even if my physical body can't leave the ground, and give me the heart of a saint, especially when the temptation to sin in anger and impatience grows strong.

Thus saith the Lord, the God of David thy father, I have heard thy prayer, I have seen thy tears: behold, I will heal thee.

— *2 Kings 20:5*

✠ ✠ ✠

Even if we feel we've been wronged by someone, if we soften our hearts and forgive the one who wronged us, the burden of bitterness will be lifted. This change is certain to affect the lives of those around us.

B e assured that if you begin, God will help you. God cannot help you unless you begin and keep on.

— Rev. Andrew Murray

O Lord, I beseech Thee, protect me from committing sin,

O Lord, help me to watch and pray,

O Lord, I give Thee thanks for what blessings I have,

O Lord, can thou deliver me from sickness, trouble and trials?

— Nancy Luce

Thus speaketh the Lord of hosts, saying, Execute true judgment, and shew mercy and compassions every man to his brother: And oppress not the widow, nor the fatherless, the stranger, nor the poor; and let none of you imagine evil against his brother in your heart.

— Zechariah 7:9–10

✠ ✠ ✠

God, the promise of your mercy is what I long for right now. With all the chaos of my day-to-day life, nothing sounds sweeter than the quiet calm of knowing you are with me always, listening and willing to forgive. I ask for the peace only your constant and enduring presence can bring. Thank you, Lord, for offering compassion no matter what my life brings.

And the Lord said unto Moses, Whosoever hath sinned against me, him will I blot out of my book. Therefore now go, lead the people unto the place of which I have spoken unto thee: behold, mine Angel shall go before thee: nevertheless in the day when I visit I will visit their sin upon them.

— *Exodus 32:33–34*

✠ ✠ ✠

The sting of rejection lingers long after it has been inflicted. It often creates an aversion to drawing near to the very thing that can bring healing: love through a relationship with God. It takes a certain willingness to risk reaching out to be forgiven by God if we ever hope to find wholeness again. But there is no more worthwhile risk than that which risks for the sake of God's love.

To the healthy, walking is a pleasure; to the sick, a burden, if not an impossibility. How many Christians there are to whom, like the maimed and the halt and the lame and the impotent, movement and progress in God's way is indeed an effort and a weariness. Christ comes to say, and with the word He gives the power, Rise and walk.

— Rev. Andrew Murray

Wherefore gird up the loins of your mind, be sober, and hope to the end for the grace that is to be brought unto you at the revelation of Jesus Christ; As obedient children, not fashioning yourselves according to the former lusts in your ignorance: But as he which hath called you is holy, so be ye holy in all manner of conversation; Because it is written, Be ye holy; for I am holy.

— 1 Peter 1:13–16

✠ ✠ ✠

God, I do not intend to hurt you and others. I am not always sure what happens in those times when I do hurt you and others. I am thankful that you forgive. Please help others to forgive me, too. Remind us all to follow your teachings. We pray that you will guide and comfort us.